Goaltending

Best Practices for Success with Setting
and Achieving Personal Goals

M. Richard Hodges

GOALFAQS PRESS
www.goalfaqs.com

Published by:
GoalFAQs Press
86 Wood Street
Milton, MA 02186
Visit our website at www.goalfaqs.com

ISBN-13: 978-0615533407
ISBN-10: 061553340X

For Allie

INTRODUCTION

An ancient Eastern proverb says, "Give a man a fish and you'll feed him for a day; teach a man to fish and you'll feed him for a lifetime."

This proverb embodies the purpose of *Goaltending*. Whether you already have an explicitly defined personal goal or simply wish to foster greater success in your life, there are time-tested practices to help you achieve these ends. These practices are not secrets known only to a few. As you read about them, you'll realize they are so common, so fundamental, to the human experience that you may be underwhelmed. But don't be deceived. The process of learning things usually requires revisiting the fundamentals in order to truly understand and effectively apply them.

Borrowing a fundamental from another discipline—journalism—this text examines what I refer to as the five best practices for success with setting and achieving personal goals. The fundamental is the "5W1H" method of newsgathering, and the acronym 5W1H stands for the following critical questions reporters ask themselves when covering a news story:

- Who?
- Why?
- What?
- When?
- Where?
- How?

A Simple But Powerful Tool

The 5W1H method of newsgathering is a simple but powerful tool for establishing not only the basic details of a news event, but also for tackling important issues a news story must be ready to answer—issues like causality and implications.

Using the 5W1H method in the context of personal goal setting and achievement, you'll benefit from asking the following questions about your goal:

- Who will do it?
- Why do it?
- What to do?
- When and where to do it?
- How did it go?

Asking and honestly answering each of these simple questions will elicit straightforward answers you can easily process and act on. What's more, the source of each of these questions contains profound truths that, when leveraged, will benefit you and your aim.

The Five Best Practices

Using one word apiece to define them, the five best practices and the 5W1H questions they respond to are:

- Empowerment (which answers the question *Who?*)
- Alignment (which answers the question *Why?*)
- Conception (which answers the question *What?*)
- Execution (which answers the questions *When?* and *Where?*)
- Evaluation (which answers the question *How?*)

As I've already suggested, you can harness these practices to your benefit. And, no matter how ordinary they may seem, they also have the uncanny ability to surprise you time-and-again with new insights about you and your ability to accomplish great things.

On the Shoulders of Giants

My awareness of these practices came about during my own pursuit for answers to questions concerning self-development in general and success with goal setting and achievement in particular. I've invested time and money over the years to uncover those answers, but, despite my writing about them here, I must confess that I very much still remain a student of them. Awareness of something isn't synonymous with mastery of it.

Isaac Newton once said, "If I have seen further than others, it is because I was standing on the shoulders of giants." Human understanding—what we often refer to as wisdom—has been passed down from generation to generation. No one man is responsible for accumulating this wisdom; instead, it's wisdom that accumulates men.

I am profoundly indebted to the many writers and thinkers whose words and ideas have shaped what I will now sketch from this vantage point. Please consider what I'm writing on these practices as notes—notes on insights I've gained from others and what has been revealed to me from my own experiences.

My hope is that reading these notes will convince you to climb a little higher and perhaps see a little further.

Goaltending

The title *Goaltending* is neither an accident nor a stab at coming up with something clever. Take it literally. Goals are like sheep that wander or gardens that grow over. Each needs tending to.

I think of goaltending as more art than science because achieving results using these five best practices is hardly scientific or formulaic. Anything "scientific" requires empirical evidence from trials whose outcomes are predictable and reproducible. In reality, each person's native intelligence, aptitudes, knowledge, skills, experience, and a host of other qualities will strongly influence the outcomes he or she experiences with a personal goal. This means that tending to one's goals is a personal—and therefore subjective—process and not one that's "one-size-fits-all."

Fortunately, these practices are rooted deeply enough in the shared human experience that they should serve each of us well. Accordingly, they remain timeless and universal, and their application in the course of setting and achieving your personal goals will undoubtedly profit you.

Summing Up the Five Best Practices

What follows is an overview of the five best practices. The chapters that follow will elaborate on each one in further detail.

<u>Empowerment</u>

Empowerment represents your acquisition of personal control over your life and the circumstances that define it. Accountability—the approach of assuming responsibility for that which happens—is a common trait among those who succeed with their goals. Therefore:

Be accountable and accept responsibility for being the causal force in your life. Being the cause in your life represents your potential to determine the effect as well.

<u>Alignment</u>

Whenever we speak of a car or golf swing as being "out of alignment," we mean that realignment will result in greater balance. The same is true with a goal. If you set out to achieve something that doesn't hold purpose for you, you'll suffer both imbalance and poor results. Therefore:

Success comes from personal goals aligned with purpose representing strengths, priorities, and values.

Conception

Well-conceived ideas and intentions represent the DNA of success. A concept is a good starting point, but it also has to fit you snugly like a suit. Just as any good suit starts with the right measurements, materials, and tailoring, so does a good goal. Therefore:

To be successful, your goals should be well-conceived, which includes being clear, specific, and modeled on previous success.

Execution

Good ideas without action are essentially worthless. It's common to have the best of intentions but still fail to follow through. In fact, two basic qualities distinguish those who dream and achieve from those who merely dream: getting started and never quitting. Therefore:

Take action with a willingness to press on no matter what.

Evaluation

Tracking and evaluating progress (or lack of progress) with your goal provides reinforcement for going the distance. Such awareness fuels greater productivity. It also affirms what you've done right and provides the opportunity to correct (and learn from) what you've done wrong. Therefore:

Consistently monitor your efforts and you'll see positive results. Realizing these results will then contribute to future success.

Why All Five

At this point you may ask yourself whether *all* five of these practices are required for successfully achieving your goal. Not necessarily, but don't take this concession as license to ignore these practices.

Imagine how difficult it is to set and achieve a goal as fantastic as running a marathon or buying a starter home. You may achieve the goal *in spite of* abandoning responsibility; or taking on something that lacks personal meaning; or failing to adequately plan the work or take meaningful action; or not bothering to assess what's been done right or wrong. You may, but somehow I doubt you'll be able to repeat it or even do it well the first time around if you ignore any one (or more) among the five.

I truly believe that contemplating the *counterfactual*— that is, predicting what would occur in the absence of one or several of these practices—should provide enough evidence to compel you to include each of them in your endeavors.

I hope you'll be able to read all of this text in one sitting as inspiration for wherever you are in the goal setting-achievement process. My own goal for this undertaking has been to be as clear, concise, practical, and informative as possible. When finished reading, I hope you'll feel I've succeeded.

M. Richard Hodges
www.goaltending.org
September 2011

NOTE TO THE READER

Throughout this text, I have used examples of various goals, such as those related to personal finance and fitness, to illustrate more general points. Because I wanted this text to be universal in its applicability, I refrained from using just one or two examples when greater diversity seemed more effective. Please do not consider this text as an authority on any of the sample goals cited—if you want to pursue a goal linked to any of their respective areas, you'll be better served by consulting the kind of specialized literature and expert advice I mention as essential for planning. To find out more information, please visit www.goaltending.org.

CHAPTER 1

Empowerment

"I know of no more encouraging fact than the unquestionable ability of man to elevate his life by conscious endeavor."

- Henry David Thoreau

Your Most Valuable Asset

In financial terms, what do you consider to be your most valuable asset?

Your home?

Or perhaps a portfolio of stocks or a retirement plan?

Or maybe a business you've bootstrapped from scratch?

Or perhaps the answer is *you*.

Think about it. If you take the income you currently earn and add to it your future earning potential for every year for the rest of your life, you'll likely find that you are worth more than any *thing* you might possess.

The fact is it all starts with you.

A Form of Self-Investment

Are you willing to invest in your most valuable asset?

Sadly, Americans today are worse at investing in their future than practically any time in modern history. For instance, in 2005 the average household savings rate dipped *below* zero percent—the first time that's happened since the Great Depression!

Don't neglect yourself the same way. Instead, invest in yourself and your quality of life by such means as preserving health, acquiring more education, and expanding your base of knowledge and skills.

Consider the following:

- The average income of someone with a bachelor's degree is almost triple that of someone else with no high school diploma. (Earning a doctorate is literally even smarter—the Ph.D. will, on average, earn five times more than the high school dropout.)

- Medical research indicates those who maintain active lifestyles decrease their risk of developing heart disease—one of the most preventable chronic conditions—by almost 50 percent.

- Researchers at Princeton University recently reported the positive relationship between income and happiness that plateaus around $75,000 per year, signifying that monetary gains are only one way of enhancing quality of life.

From here out, let's think of success in terms of you and your quality of life. That's where goals and self-investment come into play—enhancing your well-being by getting you from where you are to where you want to be.

The Power of Choice

Goals require you to not just assess where you are at present and where you want to be in the future; they also require you to make the proverbial first step of a "thousand-mile journey." Making that first step requires you to choose and be accountable for those choices.

Doing so is empowering. You've probably heard the expression "With great power comes great responsibility." But turn it on its head and witness the shift in emphasis: "With great responsibility comes great power."

Empowerment means taking on the complete package. It's value-neutral, which means that success is not always assured. As a result, the power to choose and the responsibility that comes with it will have pros and cons. If you succeed, you'll own that. If you fail, you'll own that too.

Football as a Metaphor for Life

A cynic may question how much choice (and thus power) we really have in life. I believe the answer is more than we are led to believe. Two football stories help explain why.

One day, after a particularly stinging defeat and poor performance by his team, NFL coaching legend Bill Parcells famously quipped, "You are who you are."

He was right; his players were mediocre that day. But Parcells didn't mean his players had poor abilities—the caliber of athleticism required to make it to the NFL made that impossible. Instead, he was making a statement about their lack of effort and hence their lack of accountability.

Another NFL legend, Hall of Fame halfback Gale Sayers, once described a conversation he and teammates had the evening before an important game. Sayers recalled their discussion concerned whether God plays a role in the final score of each contest. According to Sayers, the group eventually concluded that God did not, but they also agreed that God did expect every man to play up to his God-given potential.

This illustrates how much power we really do possess. We many not always get to choose the situation but we sure as hell get to choose how we respond.

Roads Taken... and Not Taken

In essence, life is all about the choices we make.

Accountability means we get to do the choosing, rather than letting circumstances—or other people or fate—do the choosing for us.

If you feel your life sucks, take accountability right now for changing that fact. If you don't like the direction in which you're heading, change course—and if you do not, acknowledge the consequences for failing to do so.

You're probably familiar with Robert Frost's well-loved poem "The Road Not Taken." Its narrator faces a dilemma—whether to travel down one path more predictable... or to take the other one less traveled by. Choosing the latter, he says, made all the difference.

Imagine if every fork in your life's series of roads represented a similar choice—to stroll down an easier path in the direction of "no" versus one uphill representing "yes." And imagine if you opted for "yes" more often than would have come naturally, especially "yes" in the context of your goals—those times when the alarm clock buzzed or deadlines loomed but begged to be postponed or when distractions and trivial time-wasters came a-calling?

Where would you be today instead of where you are now? How would your life be different?

Writing Style and Success

One of the cardinal rules of good writing is to favor the active voice over the passive. Here's a classic example:

Mistakes were made. (Passive)
I made mistakes. (Active)

You'll notice that the sentence using the active voice required an actor ("I") to whom responsibility for the verb's action ("made") could be attributed. Meanwhile, the sentence in the passive voice avoided this responsibility.

The virtue of the active voice is its emphasis on accountability—the same accountability related to choice. Consider the following goal scripts and how a goal-setter can rewrite them from something timid to something bold:

The taxes need to be filed. (Passive)
I need to file the taxes. (Active)

The house needs to be repaired. (Passive)
I need to make repairs to the house. (Active)

The business plan needs to be organized and written. (Passive)
I need to organize and write the business plan. (Active)

Reviewing these examples, it should be apparent why the active voice plays an important role in goals—using it makes someone (i.e., you) accountable!

With goals, always favor the active voice over the passive.

Someone Has to Make It Happen

The American philosopher and writer Ralph Waldo Emerson coined the term *causationist* to describe one who takes responsibility for influencing the outcomes in his or her life. (Conversely, a *determinist* yields all such responsibility to circumstance and other external forces). Because they believe and act upon the conviction that *they* are the causal force in their lives, causationists embody the spirit of well-known inspirational sayings such as "Someone has to make it happen" and "If it's to be, it's up to me."

Causationists take the initiative and don't expect handouts or bailouts. They assume accountability for their successes *and* their failures. They rarely offer excuses. When they make mistakes, causationists learn, adapt, and move on.

Knowing the Difference

Should you *really* assume responsibility for everything that happens in your life?

Of course not. There will always be some things over which you exercise little or no control. But for everything you cannot control, there is much more you can. Your health and diet, your finances, your fitness, and other factors are almost always within your power to choose or influence for better or worse.

The increased influence causationists possess in this regard is directly related to the added responsibilities they assume. Contrast their odds of success with those of determinists who opt for passivity and hence serve as bystanders in their own lives. Instead of playing a part in their life's act, determinists sit with the audience, watching everything that unfolds but ultimately having no say in how the story ends.

In the final analysis, there's no question that luck, chance, and other factors and forces beyond our control will impact our lives. Obviously, bad things happen to good people every day. Why these things happen is really outside our concern.

As needed, we can come to terms with such lack of control through spiritual or contemplative practices like meditation and prayer. One of my favorites is theologian Reinhold Niebuhr's *Serenity Prayer*, which reads in part, "God, grant me the serenity to accept the things I cannot change, the courage to change the things I can, and the wisdom to know the difference."

An Opportunity

Goals are future-oriented and have little to do with the past beyond the motivations or reasons the past serves for those goals. For example, poor diet and little to no exercise often precede personal fitness goals just as poor credit and mounting debt precede personal finance goals.

If you are haunted by the past, take this advice: *make peace with it.* Those pages have been written. Goals are about redemption and the pages you'll soon be writing.

President Kennedy once observed that, when written, the Chinese word for "crisis" is composed of two characters—one meaning "danger," the other "opportunity." (The word "crisis" itself comes from the ancient Greek word for crossroads. Two roads, one choice.)

You may feel a slight pang of anxiety when confronting (and answering) the question "Who?" but also remember that choosing accountability yields more than just responsibility. It also offers opportunity—opportunity for growth, opportunity for redemption. How empowering!

Remember, with great responsibility comes great power.

CHAPTER 2

Alignment

"No wind favors him who has no destined port."
- Michel de Montaigne

Because It's There

A reporter once asked British mountaineer George Mallory what motivated him to keep trying in his obsessive quest to summit Mount Everest.

Mallory pondered the question before offering a simple reply that has since become the stuff of legend: "Because it's there."

Love Yourself

What's the motivation for your goal? "Doing it for you" should be chief among them.

Sound too selfish or self-absorbed? Nuts. As French wit Nicholas de Chamfort aptly put it, "If you must love your neighbor as yourself, it is at least as fair to love yourself as your neighbor."

So love yourself. Not self-love in a prideful way but instead as a form of self-respect and high self-esteem. As the airplane emergency precaution instructs, you must don your own oxygen mask before you can begin to think clearly about helping others with theirs.

Too often, people recklessly deny their own needs and they pay a price for doing so. High blood pressure, stress, depression, and other ill effects are typical costs borne by an inauthentic life. The consequence is imbalance of the worst kind, a kind of high-wire act in the face of headwinds that drains life-energy.

As pleasing as pleasing others—including those you love—may be, *you must first be true to yourself.* Their happiness will not necessarily coincide with yours, nor do they have to live with the consequences of your actions— but you do.

So align your goal with personal purpose. Doing so, you'll establish a solid base from which to summit your own "mountain."

Purpose

The Kennedy Center Honors serves as America's annual tribute to the best and brightest among performing arts legends. It's a national celebration of a select few whose careers have impacted our culture in some way.

For most of the honorees, the award is a capstone moment. Despite their hard and often lonely struggles along the road to fame and success, each managed to stay at or near the top of his or her game *for decades*.

I'm convinced that a common denominator in their collective success has been the fact that these men and women were all causationists in some form or fashion. In other words, they worked hard to turn the odds in their favor.

They were also adept at realizing their dreams. Beyond assuming personal accountability, they conceived and nurtured unique visions and persistently acted on them.

But undertaking those ventures also required cultivating the endowments and talents that ultimately defined them: Bob Dylan and his lyrics, Martha Graham and her dance, Bill Cosby and his wit.

In short, they found and followed their purpose.

You possess the same capacity for cultivating your own unique endowments and talents. Or perhaps you simply have a desire to make a change in your life for the better. Or maybe there's the pursuit of something as simple as a hobby or as epic as a new career.

All of these relate to the practice of alignment, which comes from fulfilling one or more categories of purpose: *strengths*, *priorities*, and *values*.

Strengths

When someone describes you as having a particular *forte*, they're simply saying "strength" in another language.

Bestselling author and "strengths" researcher Marcus Buckingham defines a strength as "any activity that makes you feel strong." This doesn't necessarily mean a strength is something you're good at. Many of us are technically good at things that nonetheless leave us feeling weaker.

Plying your strengths will come as easy and feel as natural as writing with your dominant hand. When expressed, these strengths will also feel like simultaneous experiences of withdrawal *and* deposit of life-energy (using fuel while receiving fuel); will aid concentration and focus; and may even induce a Nirvana-like state where time will seem to stop even as it flies by. Collectively, these experiences and states are often referred to as being "on," "in the zone," or in "flow."

If you run really fast and find doing so invigorating, that's a strength. So is an ability to communicate well with others, as long as the act of doing so energizes you. There are countless examples of strengths you may possess but chances are you already know them. Buckingham asserts that your strengths become more apparent, more enhanced, and more natural as you grow more into whom you're meant to be. (Think of the infinite complexity of a massive oak tree that at one time was packed with potential as an acorn.) For strength practitioners, purposefully fulfilling this potential is liberating because there is no resistance, no inhibition, no aimlessness.

Given these advantages strengths provide, consider whether your goal will capitalize on one or more of your strengths.

Priorities

Your strengths are endowments that start with where you are. But there is another side to the coin: where you want to be. Priorities usually enter in this picture.

Priorities are the itches that need scratches.

Perhaps you've noticed more fat on your body than you'd like. Or perhaps you're considering a career change. These are typical examples of priorities. The world won't end if they're not addressed, but they are important nonetheless.

Unlike strengths, which remain fundamentally unchanged throughout one's lifetime, priorities are constantly evolving. Your priorities at age 70 are likely much different from those you had at age 20. Half a century later, you are the same person… but let's face it. You really aren't. Indeed, as you have changed over that time, so too have your priorities. This is especially obvious in the role of parents. The priorities of a new mother or father are much different than the childless adult.

Consider it this way: Strengths provide the ship you're given to sail to your goals; priorities provide the port of call. Given your current priorities, could any of them inspire a goal? If so, sail to them.

Values

Unlike goals that solely leverage strengths or respond to priorities, those based on values are driven by an agenda of doing "the right thing."

Maybe you'd like to be a better husband or wife or parent. Perhaps you'd like to give back to your community, church, or synagogue. Or maybe you'd like to enter politics or some other form of public service because you view doing so as noble.

Like priorities, values are associated with where you want to be rather than where you're starting. But unlike the "sudden necessity" or adaptability of priorities, values represent something more permanent. Serving a higher purpose, they are timeless and enduring.

Reflect on whether your goal may be one rooted in such values.

The Alignment Advantage

Alignment represents you doing your best work because it's in harmony with your strengths, priorities, and values. This doesn't mean you cannot set and achieve goals that aren't purposeful. You'll just find that neither the odds nor the reward of achieving success—in both a material and psychological sense—will be as great.

In Spite of Fear

Can you recall personal goals—honest-to-goodness goals that you were once committed to—that somehow fizzled or otherwise never materialized? If you analyzed each case to uncover its reasons for failure, what would those reasons be?

One common denominator may have been fear, or more precisely, the unwillingness to assume the risk of physical or emotional harm. While fear will prey upon the determinist and causationist alike, it is the latter who shows a willingness to proceed in spite of fear.

This, and not the absence of fear, is the definition of courage.

Coping with Fear

We cannot escape fear, but we can learn to manage it.

The fear you may face with your goal could be physical—such as with phobias and panic attacks that manifest physical reactions—or emotional—such as a fear of failure, disapproval, or rejection.

There's no shame in having these fears. Indeed, they're natural responses designed to protect us from harm. The adrenaline rush associated with a "fight or flight" response is the classic example. But, unfortunately, what helped preserve us thousands of years ago has become more of a burden in the modern age where taking some (perceived) risks may be necessary.

Most fears and anxieties, when analyzed objectively, are either illogical or minimally useful. A cure for combating and exposing the irrationality of such fears is to pose a simple but provocative question: "So what?"

Repeatedly respond to each excuse with "So what?" and see how long it takes before you recognize the futility of wasted worry. After all, it doesn't make sense to let something take space in your head without paying the rent.

The sky won't fall and the worst rarely, if ever, will come to pass.

The Ultimate Risk

All worthy goals involve some form of risk, perhaps none greater or more common than the risk of being yourself and "doing your thing"—in other words, putting your ego and your effort out there for the world to judge.

Many goals perish for this reason.

There will be the occasional critic or skeptic with the "crab mentality" who will pooh-pooh your efforts. In all likelihood, they'll do so because they either resent your nerve to take command of your destiny or because your assumption of causation will force them to reexamine their own life-choices.

Ignore them. The heroes of history are the nonconformists, those who pursue their dreams in spite of skepticism and without seeking the approval of others. As the writer Richard Bach observed, "Your only obligation in any lifetime is to be true to yourself."

With a healthy understanding of your goal's purpose and the realization that most associated fears are unwarranted, you'll recognize that the risk is almost always worth the reward.

Apple Computers co-founder Steve Jobs has understood—and lived—this truth while exhorting others to do likewise. In a commencement address to graduates at Stanford University, he once said:

> Your time is limited, so don't waste it living someone else's life. Don't be trapped by dogma—which is living with the results of other people's thinking. Don't let the noise of others' opinions drown out your own inner voice. And most important, have the courage to follow your heart and intuition. They somehow already know what you truly want to become. Everything else is secondary.

CHAPTER 3

Conception

"Time is the coin of your life. It is the only coin you have, and only you can determine how it will be spent. Be careful lest you let other people spend it for you."

- Carl Sandburg

Conception

Inception

In the words of management guru Stephen Covey, all things are created twice: once in the mind, once again in reality.

Many of today's successful businesses once existed on paper only in the form of a business plan. Marathons and marathon training often begin with nothing more than a timetable of distances and intervals. And the work of great writers often begins with merely an outline.

Covey's observation has been true throughout recorded history. When the first farmers developed what we today know as agriculture, they took a risk based on the conviction that what they sowed in the springtime would reap a harvest come autumn. The ability to conceive a desired end-result guided their way. Literally, they envisioned the fruits of their labors.

The same power of imagination is necessary for goals as well. Like crops planted without any consideration or careful planning, ill-conceived goals will wither and die. They never really stand a chance when tested, even as those well-conceived go on to flourish.

Writing a Scaffold

To achieve success, your goal will need to be both clear and specific. Being otherwise vague, it's likely to produce limited results.

What's needed is a framework, a scaffold, for your goal, and clarity and specificity will help you establish this framework. Writing down (or typing) everything central to your goal—including the goal itself and the accompanying objectives that support it—takes it one step further, providing a covenant (with yourself) similar to the terms of a contract or the rules of a game. (The worksheet provided at www.goaltending.org should help you with this process.)

Research has found that writing is a useful ritual that serves a two-fold purpose: (1) nailing down in print the thoughts that otherwise sink and disappear into the deep of the mind, and (2) providing metaphoric "flesh and bone" to those thoughts, which previously exist only as emotions and symbols. As one team of researchers specializing in writing note, "we do not so much send our thoughts in pursuit of words as use words to pursue our thoughts."

As such, writing down your goal and objectives will aid your pursuit of clarity and specificity. And because it requires your full attention, composing your thoughts on paper will force you to consider these subjects in an active, rather than passive, manner.

Clarity

Clarity means being clear on every potential aspect of the vision for your goal. It's paramount in the language you use to define your goal, which is best done in the form of a sentence. You should leave nothing ambiguous.

Here are some examples of vague personal goals that could be more clear:

- I want to be rich.
- I want to have a more satisfying career.
- I want to be less fat.
- I could use a higher degree.

Each of these goals suffers from ambiguity and lack of detail. In reality, they are nothing more than intentions.

Consider the first example. How is "rich" defined—in other words, how much money would qualify as "rich"? And is money the yardstick by which to measure "rich"—or is it something else—perhaps love, friendship, or adopting a certain lifestyle?

Assume that money is the yardstick and that one million dollars would do, and you finally have something tangible on which to focus your efforts.

But even the statement "I want to earn a million dollars" doesn't have enough gas to travel far. It's still more in the sphere of intention than being a full-blown goal. As you strive for clarity, you'll also need detail—the province of specificity.

Specificity

Think of your goal as the destination, but one with specific milestones (which I'll call objectives) along the journey. Unlike your goal, which represents a desired *outcome*, objectives embody the *process* of achieving your goal. Again: one is an outcome, the other a process.

Objectives are the actionable steps that move you along the continuum between intention and achievement. If getting from start to finish is a matter of A-to-Z, then every letter in between represents a specific, actionable objective.

As an outcome, a goal will be less concrete and instead more abstract. Think of goals such as "the beach body" or "the nest egg." It's easy to conceptualize these goals, but because they are only prizes at the end of the journey, their usefulness during the process of that journey is limited to providing motivation (desire) and orientation (direction).

Objectives and their accompanying tasks (which are simply more discrete objectives within objectives) provide the grounding required for getting from where you are to where you ultimately want to be. For example, training for and running a marathon may include the following objectives (in no necessary order):

- Proper training (often daily) involving runs of various distances and paces.
- Running competitive races of various distances to prepare or qualify for the big race.
- Researching guidance on proper technique, nutrition, scheduling, etc.

Notice the details? Notice how specific each objective is? And notice how stern they are? Reading this list of examples, you might agree that goals are much sexier than objectives! (After all, everyone wants to notch the marathon on their belt—but who really feels the same way about daily training runs?) Yet without the concreteness objectives provide, a goal is simply a mirage—there one minute, gone the next.

Thomas Edison's observation that success is "10 percent inspiration and 90 percent perspiration" applies here. Goals provide the inspiration, objectives the perspiration.

But despite their "bad cop" tendencies, objectives exist to serve your best interests. Ultimately, those who fail to realize their goals are those who either lack or fail to follow through on detailed objectives. They're like ships that steer aimlessly out of port rather than charting and sailing specific courses.

Simplicity

You've probably heard the expression "keep it simple, stupid" (and its well-known acronym K.I.S.S.), which is wise advice. Indeed, we often overcomplicate things when simplicity would serve us better.

Personal goal development is often mired in the complex because we foolishly equate complexity with quality, despite the reality that the more complex a goal is, the more likely it is to fail. While amateurs typically fall into this trap, the pros know better: keep it simple and stick with the fundamentals.

Please don't confuse simplicity with lack of sophistication. A goal can be sophisticated and still achieve "beginner's mind," the perspective that induces possibilities and solutions to challenges not easily perceived in a complex world. Indeed, research has shown that too much complexity can shut down the mind's ability to process and act on decisions (a problem commonly referred to as "analysis paralysis").

While there is never a sweet spot that tells you when your goal has become too complicated, you can always ask whether it (or its objectives) can be simplified. What is unnecessary, what is excessive, what can be stripped away and not detract from the aim or purpose of the goal?

Put simply, simplify.

Feasibility

The paradox of a goal is that its objectives ought to be within reach but still border on the unreachable. In other words, your goal should be feasible but also stretch you.

A common mantra in business is to "underpromise and overdeliver." This is applicable to goals as well. By setting and exceeding realistic expectations, you manage to avoid the all-too-human tendency to over-commit out of enthusiasm or a desire to please others.

Beyond his obvious gifts as a film director, Clint Eastwood has been a good investment for the studios that finance his films because he always brings his pictures in on time and under budget. Avoiding indulgences such as extended takes in favor of an economy of style, Eastwood manages to consistently churn out Academy Award-winning and nominated films. Quality is not something lost in the process.

Emulate Eastwood's example. Set *realistic*—note that I didn't say *low*—expectations and then go on to exceed them.

Think you're ready for a marathon? Try a half-marathon first, *then* notch a marathon on your belt next time. Want to lose 10 pounds this summer? Aim for 5, then reassess and perhaps even recommit to another 5 when you're done the first go-round. You get the picture.

Flexibility

When stressed, muscle tissue will rebuild and become stronger in preparation for the next time it endures the same workload. The same concept applies to your goaltending "muscles." Upon meeting each set of feasible expectations, you'll want to recalibrate what's "feasible" because the challenge next time will not be so great.

But flexibility is not just about stretching. It's also about knowing when to remain firm as much as when to flex.

If you've established a goal that ultimately proves too ambitious, scale it back. Unforeseen circumstances or poor preparation can (and will) happen, so learn when to cut yourself slack when necessary and where warranted. Give yourself room to scale back, but don't let that stymie your efforts. If you can't put in the extra training mile or move the usual amount of money into savings, then do what's realistic. The key here is to *never lose your momentum*. Motivation is an engine that can be slowed down but should never stop.

Slippage, the tendency to carelessly give way once a way is given, can be tempting when your goal is off in the distance and all you have directly in front are brutal objectives. Slippage is the devil on your shoulder that says, "Why bother now with what can be done later?"

Resist such temptation at all costs. Flexibility is not the same as flaccidity. Doing it "later" *rarely happens*, so be careful in the choices you make.

Sustainability

The right kind of goal is a sustainable goal.

"Owning" a goal is like owning a pet. When you adopt it, you also become accountable for it. In other words, *you* are responsible when things go wrong.

Think about how irresponsible it would be to have a puppy for the cute and cuddly reasons but to ignore or avoid those less pleasant (having to scoop the poop, constantly walking it, dealing with shredded furniture or shoes, etc.).

Like owning that dog, if the prospect of doing all that your goal requires presents a problem, you may want to reconsider your ambition and perhaps even your commitment to that intention.

But also know that you should make your goal work for you as much as you work for it. This is another form of flexibility, one with an aim of enhancing sustainability. Find ways to make the seemingly unmanageable manageable. Or better yet, make it a game. And if you can't do that, at least make it as agreeable as possible. For example, if your goal is to lose weight and routinely eating a repetitive yet balanced diet works better than constantly counting calories for a diet greater in variety—substituting one form of monotony for another—then more power to you.

Measurability

Success with your goal will require evaluating how successful you've been.

The goal itself always has a simple bar to clear—whether or not you accomplished it—so everything you really measure will relate to the objectives and tasks that serve as paths to that goal.

What you are measuring (each unique measure is known as a *metric*) to gauge success with your goal will undoubtedly come from a hodge-podge of your own research, expert advice, and professional recommendations. Among the available metrics, choose and use those that seem most appropriate for you and your circumstances. Experience being the best teacher, you'll likely discover what works well and what doesn't.

You'll also come to find some metrics are more credible than others. Take weight loss for example. People often obsess over the number of pounds they weigh, but weight isn't necessarily the best metric if your goal is to have the "beach body." When pressed, you may concede that wanting the beach body is really a matter of stripping away body fat. Whether pounds are lost (perhaps for a slimmer physique) or gained (since muscle weighs more than fat), loss of body fat is really the objective at hand. Hence, percentage body fat—and not weight—would be the appropriate metric.

Metrics can be *quantitative* or *qualitative*. Quantitative metrics can be expressed numerically, including numbers (such as a diastolic/systolic blood pressure reading or the number of words written daily for a business plan) and percentages (such as a percentage of income invested in personal savings or percentage body fat). Qualitative metrics typically involve anything requiring self-inquiry along the lines of a "1-to-10" scale (such as how much "effort" you put into studying for an exam or rankings of potential career opportunities).

Whatever your goal's objectives, it's likely that others—particularly experts in the field or prior novices who now have invaluable experience and insights to share—have invested the time and resources to uncover a road-tested set of metrics, so feel free to piggyback on their experience. Otherwise, part of the challenge (and fun) of goaltending is learning through trial and error what metrics best suit you.

Timeliness

Someone once aptly described goals as dreams with deadlines. The weight of time adds a positive pressure, a sense of urgency, which provides a significant contribution to pressing the dream into reality.

Some people work well under the "tyranny" of the clock. Others do not. (Ironically, those who hate it the most probably need it most.) Regardless, time marches on. Therefore, whatever you think of time, acknowledge and respect it.

Sometimes you have your deadline as soon as you set your goal. If you want to run a marathon, you have a date by which to do it (and train for it). The beach body has its season. And retirement planning depends on when you would like to wind down a career.

But if your goal doesn't present a clear deadline, then choose one that intuitively seems right. The point is to have a very specific date, no matter how arbitrary—or hokey—that may seem. After all, many of life's deadlines are arbitrary. Why April 15th for taxes? Why the first Tuesday in November for elections?

Why not?

Modeling

Modeling presumes that your behavior is a function of your environment. "Monkey see, monkey do" is a cruder way of putting it. The benefit to you and your goal is the ability to apply modeling intentionally and choose which models you observe and therefore imitate.

We routinely model the behavior of ideal role models—known as *exemplars*—in various ways. For example, if your goal is to become a better writer, you'll likely study—and try to replicate—the patterns of behavior of great writers. Want to lose weight or get fit? Perhaps you'll emulate diets or fitness trends endorsed by experts and celebrities. The same logic applies to other pursuits as well.

A century ago, modeling was touted as a supreme key in accumulating wealth. Back then, you would have been instructed to study—and then replicate—the patterns of behavior of the rich to decode what led to their success. The case of Horatio Alger is perhaps the most famous of these "rags to riches" exemplars.

Will following an exemplar's "formula" mean you'll experience the same level of achievement? Of course not. There are limits to how far enthusiasm or determination can lead you. Yet this does not take away from the value of following in their footsteps. Indeed, ponder the alternative: How far would you go if not for their example to lead you?

But success is not solely the province of immortals. In addition to modeling the behavior of the well-known, study and emulate the success of the "average Joe." These are the "if they can do it, I can do it too" exemplars who inspire each of us to tap into our potential greatness. Remind yourself that "they" were once "you."

Hopefully, once you learn what others are capable of achieving, you'll be inspired to blaze trails as well.

Mere Words

Unfortunately, most goals stop here—with mere words. Stillborn. Lifeless.

As they say in Texas, this leaves you with "all hat and no cattle."

Millions—perhaps even billions—of people on Earth every year cross the figurative starting line on New Years Day with well-intentioned goals but soon neglect them and ultimately drop out of the race.

Don't be one of them. Remember, you possess the ability to choose differently. A worthy goal will require sacrifice; simply acknowledge that fact beforehand and remain accountable. As another saying goes, "don't let your mouth write checks your butt can't cash."

This is the theme of *execution*, which I want to talk about next.

CHAPTER 4

Execution

"A good plan violently executed now is better than a perfect plan executed next week."

- George Patton

Revealing Character

A college writing instructor once invited his former students to come to a current class to share their experiences as writers in the real world. One of those former students, John, was a reporter for the *New York Times*.

Writing, John told his audience, is not simply a matter of *being* a writer. Instead, the true writer is one who is always *doing* the things writers should be doing. In other words, writers are writers through their actions. For example, reporters undertake activities like *investigating*, *editing*, *interviewing*, and—best of all—*writing*.

The same logic applies to any activity related to your goal. Focus on the *doing* and the *being* will take care of itself.

Your objectives should help in this regard. They specify the actions to undertake: *running* (for a marathon), *saving* (for a nest egg), or *networking* (for a business). There's no riddle to it. It's simply a matter of execution.

Actors and dramatists understand this truth; "action reveals character" is a proverb in their trade. Equally true is the advice given to young legislators who are sometimes all-too-eager to change the world with platitudes and speeches rather than committee work and constituent mail: "It's better to be a workhorse than a showhorse."

Slowly, Slowly

Travel to Africa to climb Mount Kilimanjaro (the continent's highest peak), and you'll likely employ a small army of guides and porters to help you to the top. As you climb higher and higher in elevation, the oxygen becomes ever-thinner and the climbing ever-tougher. It may be then that you will hear a voice purr the Swahili phrase "pole-pole," which means "slowly, slowly."

The locals often say this because eager greenhorns will often make the ascent too hard, too quick, and burn out before completing a day's hike. Like Aesop's fable of *The Tortoise and the Hare*, the objective is solely to get to the top and not necessarily in record time.

When climbing that same mountain, I found myself constantly teetering on the brink of collapse, at which point I would choose to focus on anything, *anything*, that I could stumble to within eyeshot. Making it there, I could then recalibrate and recommit to the next visible landmark. Like threading pearls on a necklace, I focused on completing each segment until there was none left.

My point? Use incremental focus to approach your goal and its objectives likewise.

There's an old joke that asks how you eat an elephant. The answer: one piece at a time. Objectives help you "eat the elephant" that is your goal, one piece at a time. Although objectives often require steadiness, determination, and persistence, the fact is that anything complex can be "chunked" down to simple, actionable basics (hence the more specialized role of tasks within objectives).

Meanwhile, goals provide the rationale for why you're eating an elephant in the first place!

Playing Small Ball

Once you analyze the reasons for others' success, you'll discover a trend contrary to the conventional wisdom: success is not all about grand slams and walk-off home runs; it's mostly about base hits and bunts and steals and all the other things known in baseball as "small ball." In other words, success occurs incrementally. This may sound contradictory, because we usually think of (and celebrate) success in large terms.

But smart people know the difference the "little things" make. You may often hear of businesses operating "at the margins" because the margins are what make or break it. The same, consistent focus on the little things is true for goals—little things such as tasks within an objective.

Dieting requires dedication and consistency with the little things. So do saving money, starting a new career path, or planning a wedding. In other words, most worthy goals operate under this principle.

Bit-by-bit is how you too will do it. So slow down. Focus. And eat that elephant.

Finding the Time

"Making it happen" relies on you making it happen. And that means *when* you'll make it happen. Problems start when you can't (or don't) resolve *when*.

Lack of time is a common excuse these days. Work is just part of everyone's already crowded daily schedule; obligations to family, friends, and other personal priorities require time, too.

But you have to choose where your goal sits in that shuffle.

How important the goal is compared to these other competing priorities is up to you. Chances are that, by reading this book, you already have an inkling—if not an intention—of something very important to you. That's a start. Yet you're also likely wondering where to squeeze it into your daily schedule.

Here's a suggestion: 60 minutes every day at the beginning of the morning. After all, you're already conditioned to this "sacrifice" because we do it each year when we "fall back" (and lose an hour) for daylight savings time. So, when it comes to the issue of making the time, you've really got no excuse.

It's also likely you spend a decent portion of every day on essentially useless activities like watching television or surfing the Internet, time that could instead be applied more productively. Cut this "fat" out of your daily schedule and you'll find even more time for early to bed, early to rise.

Habits as Keys to Success

Given the chance, I would edit the standard dictionary entry for *habit* to read "consistency in your walk meeting your talk." Such a definition places habit at the intersection of not only conception and execution but also repetition (a best practice for success that I've omitted from the list of five but which nonetheless deserves honorable mention).

If you want to really bust through a goal, find something that works and then turn to it again and again and *again*. Consistent repetition (of what works) just may be the master-skill for getting you from where you are to where you want to be.

The following are some examples of common denominators of the "successful" (those who achieve their goals) that can be characterized as reproducible habits:

- The successful tend to be early risers and judicious with how they manage their time each day.
- The successful are persistent and consistent; they establish and remain faithful to rules they set for themselves and rarely, if ever, break them.
- The successful take the time to plan and contemplate the outcomes of their actions, but they're never paralyzed by such analysis.
- The successful recognize that perfection is never possible and, therefore, accept a tolerable level of imperfection in all that they do.
- The successful practice affirmations and positivity-centered techniques such as visualization of success with their goals.

- The successful study and apply the lessons of each failure they experience.

But remember—habits are only habits if you apply and stick with them. To quote something that *is* in the dictionary, you must *inculcate* good habits. (The word "inculcate" comes from the Latin root *calcare*, which means "to trample"—ponder that.)

As Aristotle observed, "We are what we repeatedly do. Excellence, then, is not an act but a habit."

Procrastination

"Why do today what can be done tomorrow?" is the procrastinator's twist on the more reasonable "Never put off till tomorrow what can be done today."

Because of its instant gratification effect, procrastination is like a drug. Being human, we are always prey to its temptations. Acknowledging this, here are some recommended strategies for squarely addressing procrastination:

- **Don't delay.** Recognize exactly what it is you are procrastinating about and then commit to doing it *right away.* Motivational speaker and author Brian Tracy refers to this strategy as "Eat that Frog!" The idea is that once you resolve the source of the delay, you won't be saddled by the drain on personal energy that comes from avoidance. Then, with the rest of the day free to do more productive things, you'll be at your best.

- **Reward yourself.** Find ways to reward yourself for completing tasks that lead to completing objectives and, consequently, the goal itself. A delayed gratification strategy will keep you hungry and less inclined to sloth—unlike the less coherent strategy of reward now, work later.

- **Leverage the negative.** Studies have shown that, on average, people respond more strongly to a negative stimulus than a positive one of the same magnitude. For example, losing $100 at a Blackjack table represents more in terms of "pain" than winning

$100 does in terms of "pleasure." To leverage this finding to your benefit, find creative ways to install negative consequences for failures to meet set objectives or tasks. For example, you might announce your personal goal to others and request they regularly check in and keep you honest. Or try using financial incentives—such as "fines" in the form of donations to politicians or causes you find reprehensible—to increase your odds of taking action.

- **Acknowledge your fear.** Psychologist and author Neil Fiore asserts that we procrastinate for one reason: it rewards us with temporary relief from stress. As mentioned before, some form of fear— whether it's a fear of imperfection, failure, change, or commitment—can manifest, often when you're most vulnerable. Do your best to analyze what fear (or fears) may exist, why it exists, and then proceed to "pop the balloon" of irrationality it represents.

- **Contain procrastination.** All work and no play make Jack a dull boy, right? Then perhaps you should consider a strategy of containment rather than futilely attempting to eliminate procrastination altogether. Fiore's recommended solution? Recognize the need for downtime we often require to decompress from life's daily struggles and add it to your schedule of priorities. By holding out a portion of your day or week for leisure and frivolous activities, you'll no longer be able to justify the temptation to indulge a "quick fix" that otherwise has no outlet.

Persistence

If you ever wonder why stores and manufacturers offer ridiculous rebates "too-good to be true," the answer is simple: they know the probability of who will take the time and effort to respond and those who won't. In other words, they predict (and thereby count on) a certain portion of eligible customers to be too lazy to follow a few simple instructions.

Remember, in the world of business, *the house usually wins*. Rebates are not a charity, so those who offer them only do so with the unwitting consent of lazy consumers.

But imagine how the process would be different if each consumer demonstrated persistence.

Your goal requires that same willingness to carry through what's necessary and not quit. Obviously, the sacrifices involved—time, energy, money—are far greater than clipping a proof-of-purchase and mailing in a form.

But like the rebate, you repeatedly have the option to *do it* or *not do it* with your goal. It's your choice. Just don't be predictable.

The Wisdom of Failure

Pursuing your personal goal will involve a constant series of "tests" of persistence. Fundamentally, these tests ask whether you have the will to keep going in spite of every setback and failure along the way. Having sufficient desire and the wisdom to learn from these failures are the keys to passing these tests.

Have you ever set out to do something, received a blow or setback of some kind along the way, and immediately quit out of frustration? If so, it's likely you never had sufficient desire in the first place. Or, if quitting took place after several attempts, perhaps the desire was there but you simply lacked the wisdom to learn from previous mistakes.

IBM founder Thomas Watson was once quoted as saying that success is found "on the far side of failure." His observation is embodied in the apocryphal account of Thomas Edison's chronic failures to create the light bulb— until one day he succeeded. It is said that Edison made a thousand failed attempts before finally achieving his goal. When asked how it felt to endure so many mistakes, Edison replied: "I didn't fail a thousand times. It just happened to be a thousand-step process."

So press on, even in spite of failure. In the words of Calvin Coolidge:

> Nothing can take the place of persistence. Talent will not; the world is full of unsuccessful people with talent. Genius will not; unrewarded genius is almost a proverb. Education alone will not; the world is full of educated derelicts. Persistence and determination alone are omnipotent.

CHAPTER 5

Evaluation

"Perfection is not attainable, but if we chase perfection we can catch excellence."

- Vince Lombardi

How Are You Doing?

Of all the 5W1H method questions, one remains: *how*—as in *how are you doing?*

The answer will be informed by the goal-related information you track and evaluate. Just as a flame needs oxygen, self-evaluation requires details—details concerning what you did (and what you did not do).

Tracking such details shouldn't be complicated. Any means will likely do—it can be as simple as using an index card or spiral notebook or as complicated as maintaining a computer spreadsheet or database. Contrary to what Marshall McLuhan said, the medium is not the message.

As noted before, goal-related metrics involve the careful selection and monitoring of specific kinds of details, which, for simplicity, I'll refer to hereafter as *data*. Evaluating this data in the context of your goal has three particularly redeeming qualities: *objectivity*, *awareness*, and *automation*.

Objectivity

Being human, we are often subject to bias when asked to make an evaluation without having data to back up our assertions. It's even worse when we evaluate ourselves. The result is a tendency to overemphasize the positives and minimize the negatives, a phenomenon known as *fundamental attribution error.*

A common example of fundamental attribution error occurs when people are asked to assess the values of their homes. Try it: If you currently own a home, how much do you think it's worth? Now how much do you think your home is worth to a potential buyer—could looking at the price of comparable home sales in the area help you determine the answer? (Yes, according to banks, insurance brokers, and real estate agents.)

But chances are the two figures won't be nearly anywhere close to one another. Because of fundamental attribution error, most of us will unconsciously inflate the value of our homes (remember all the "sweat equity" you put into it over the years?). In fact, from an objective (data-based) standpoint, the value of your home should, in all likelihood, reflect several variables beyond the home itself, including the value of homes in the surrounding area but also macro-trends like the overall liquidity of the housing market and the ability of banks to lend.

In truth, we can't trust ourselves to objectively judge ourselves. Data solves this problem. Data is indifferent and won't "fudge." Calories counted, miles run, and doors knocked on are all examples of goal-related data that would otherwise be prey to fundamental attribution error if not tracked by some honest broker. These numbers are not capable of lying, even if you are.

Awareness

Drop a frog in a pot of boiling water and he'll hop right out.

Drop him in the water while it's lukewarm and he'll lie there. Then, as you *slowly* turn up the heat, he'll boil thoroughly without knowing his fate is cooked.

Too often, each of us is as numb—and dumb—as that frog about where we stand in terms of progressing along our goal's journey from an intention to an achievement. It may not seem like a problem but this lack of awareness can often go overboard. It's like taking a hike in the woods but winding up lost with no map or compass to get back. You never planned to go astray, but it's usually only when you've gotten *really* lost that you realize how bad you've let things go. Indeed, it sometimes takes the thud of hitting rock bottom to truly understand the depths to which you've sunk.

What's needed is a way to maintain awareness. That's where tracking data becomes invaluable. Consistently monitor your efforts and you'll see positive results. This is embodied in Peter Drucker's famous observation that "what gets measured gets managed."

By stimulating your interest and helping you comprehend exactly what you've accomplished, your goal's metrics will keep you as aware and on task as a hiker with a map and compass—or, better yet, a GPS.

And just think—armed with a thermometer, the frog would have been aware, too, knowing just when to make his escape.

Automation

Living in the twenty-first century, we're fortunate to have access to many tools (some might say toys) to assist with automating the data tracking process. For example, heart rate monitors, pedometers, body fat scales, and other devices facilitate the automatic tracking of progress with fitness and health-related goals. Computer software, notably Microsoft Excel, also makes it easy to plug in numbers for a variety of metrics, such as the number of words written daily (useful for aspiring authors) and money saved towards a down payment on a mortgage (useful for aspiring homeowners).

The purpose of automation is to have a some form of logging mechanism take on the task of what is usually more complicated than you as a human being can process or retain. The joy of the modern age is that portable electronic devices (such as smart phones) contain a wealth of bells and whistles: built-in calendars and automatic notifications, GPS tracking, calorie counters, and a host of other available applications tailored to the needs of your goal, making tracking a breeze and, even better, automatic.

Garbage In, Garbage Out

The various methods available for self-evaluation share one thing in common—all require good data.

As it refers to data, the expression "garbage in, garbage out" (GIGO) provides a useful reminder that your input influences your output. In other words, bad data will misinform evaluative efforts and thus lead to misinformation and, consequently, poor choices.

Conversely, the insights that good data can reveal—patterns of success, the value of alternatives, and the power of incentives—really matter and may even surprise. Businesses understand this. They constantly evaluate marketing data to anticipate potential opportunities; sales and revenue data to know which products and services to expand; and data concerning competitor activity to calibrate future strategy.

What works for business will work for you and your personal goal, too.

Consider three relatively simple forms of evaluation that you can apply when assessing data related to your goal: *degree of difference*, *course correction*, and *quality assurance*.

Degree of Difference

Minding "the gap" between where you are and where you want to be is simply a matter of assessing a difference. Taking stock of that difference along the way will be key to establishing the *degree of difference* that exists, and it's the degree of difference that typically serves witness to change.

(Here's a tip: Before you start your goal, you should "take a snapshot" of data representing your status prior to any action so you can later evaluate how far you've come along. This is known as a *baseline* measurement. For example, if your goal is to reduce body fat, a baseline body fat percentage will aid in later assessing any progress you've made.)

Absolute difference considers the magnitude (size) of difference independent of anything else. In other words, the difference is measured incrementally. For example, your objective may be to reduce your percentage body fat to 20 percent. In this case, the difference from whatever percentage body fat you're starting from at baseline is irrelevant because all that concerns you is hitting 20 percent—nothing more, hopefully less. As a result, you'll often focus your evaluative efforts on the number of body fat percentage points left until achieving your goal. Typical examples of metrics related to absolute difference might include getting back into a certain size of jeans or fundraising a pre-specified amount of money.

Relative difference represents one metric value in terms of another. For example, your running pace today compared to the one called for by your training schedule, which would be a difference expressed in relative (or comparative) terms. Or consider comparing your metric with that of a teammate or partner or even yourself from an earlier time period.

Unlike absolute difference, relative difference can be expressed in terms of a percentage or ratio because you have two figures with which to calculate the difference. (Relative difference is especially useful for making apples-to-apples comparisons—like how my pace improvement fared in comparison to yours.)

Here are some simple examples to illustrate how this works:

- **Absolute difference.** If you drafted a business plan that called for raising $10,000 to cover start-up expenses, you'll want to monitor, each day, how much more money to raise before reaching your target. Perhaps that gap can be broken into discrete daily targets to make the overall process more manageable—if so, you'll still mind the gap, but on a daily basis in which you "don't quit it until you get it."
- **Relative difference.** If previous fundraising efforts earned $10,000 for a non-profit but an improved strategy later yielded $15,000, you would have experienced a 50 percent improvement. In this case, the relative difference of 50 percent may be more important (as opposed to a $5,000 bump in earnings) because you're wanting to "yardstick" how you did compared to an earlier performance.

If you hate statistics, relax. Just remember to keep it simple. When tracking and evaluating your goals, *stick to what are considered simple gold-standard metrics* and familiarize yourself with whether they are assessed incrementally (in absolute terms) or comparatively (in relative terms). That way, you'll do well with minding the gap.

Course Correction

Did you know that airline pilots often have little to do for the bulk of their journeys? Instead, given a point of departure and a set destination, a computer will devise flight plans with coordinates that account for the shortest possible distance (good weather permitting) along with the knowledge of flight paths of nearby aircraft.

Despite such precision, the flight itself is another matter. External forces such as wind and turbulence diverge the plane from its "straight as the crow flies" path. If the computer did not constantly recalibrate the flight, a transatlantic trip to London could just as easily end up in Lisbon!

This periodic adjustment is known as a *course correction*, and the practice of evaluation provides the same opportunity to assess where you are relative to your goal's intended course. When you "blow" off course, your data will tell you. Simply recalibrate and invest your energies into returning to your goal's "flight path."

Course correction is a particularly important form of evaluation given how precious (and finite) a resource time is. You may have a seemingly unlimited source of motivation to go on and on, but you've only got so much time—thus the importance of remaining on target.

Quality Assurance

Quality assurance—or simply "QA"—does not entail evaluating goal-related data. Instead, QA is a means of examining the ways by which data is produced and collected as well as examining your use of the five best practices for goaltending. While QA will not always reveal problems, it will provide a useful "audit" of whether they exist.

Here are some basic questions to consider employing in QA:

- *Are you using the best approach?* If you aren't accomplishing objectives as soon as expected, perhaps there are more viable alternatives.
- *Are you using the optimal metric(s)?* Experts advise using the more appropriate metric of percentage body fat rather than weight if the goal is to improve appearance. Are there analogous examples that may apply to your goal?
- *Are you sticking with best practices?* In other words, are you assuming accountability? Are you pursuing goals aligned with your strengths, priorities, and values? Have you spent the necessary time fleshing out your goal concept so that it is clear, specific, measurable, and so forth? Finally, have you taken sufficient action to complete the objectives and tasks necessary for achieving your goal?

On Quitting

And then there's quitting. How do you evaluate that which is incomplete?

Should this happen, reflect on what went wrong and why. Understanding those reasons and learning their lessons will only benefit you in future attempts to get back in the saddle.

One reason for quitting may have been too much ambition. If so, determine whether it was a matter of too much, too soon, or perhaps both. Insufficient time to realize true progress can lead to frustration when in fact you've made subtle improvements that would be more obvious given a longer timeframe. Likewise, too much early on can lead to otherwise avoidable burnout. Recall the proverb that you must first learn to crawl before you can walk or even run.

Perhaps lack of progress can be traced to poor methods or inadequate objectives. QA will hopefully help you recognize this. A typical example is the failure to use proper form when lifting weights. There are literally scores of books and guides that illustrate how to lift properly, but that doesn't mean that everyone can artfully execute what appears simple on paper. (This raises an important point regarding the need for expert help in certain cases: If self-instruction isn't working—regardless of whether your goal involves physical activity—you may need to rely on a more specialized or personalized form of instruction.)

Perhaps there's something beyond your control that's affecting your results. A bad economy may hinder plans to save income, just as a serious illness may inhibit training necessary for a 10-K. In such cases, accept what you cannot control and focus on what you can. If you have to wait until things settle down to start over and try again, so be it.

Whatever the reason for incomplete or inadequate progress, the key to remember is that failure is only failure if you fail to learn from it. Otherwise, trust that where you are will eventually lead to a "tipping point" to greater success.

When to Evaluate

When and how often should you evaluate? It depends. Ultimately, answering that question will rely on factors specific to your goal and your circumstances, but keep the following in mind:

- Be consistent about when you evaluate and make sure the intervals are spread out evenly to avoid skewing results.
- Make each evaluation infrequent enough to establish clear definition between results but frequent enough to effectively course correct.
- Consider the time you reserve for evaluating as sacred and therefore deserving performance in a space that's quiet, avoids all distractions, and promotes thinking and reflection.

Reactivity

Psychologists use the term *reactivity* to describe the phenomenon of individuals under observation altering their behavior in response to an awareness that they're being monitored.

Knowing that someone else could be observing you, would you act differently? What if the observation was related to your goal—would you perform better or worse?

For better or worse, the fact is that we behave differently under the eyes of another. Whether that's a good or bad thing is irrelevant. What is relevant is your opportunity to leverage reactivity to your advantage.

Who will observe your progress as you proceed with your goal? Most likely you and no one else. But it's not really *you* in the present tense. It's another you. A future you. This alternate you is constantly monitoring every opportunity you have to match your walk to your talk. When it speaks, it provides what some call "the radio voice in your head." Consider it your conscience, the one that has to pay tomorrow for the mistakes you make today. It's the you that cares because it's the you that will ultimately pay the tab.

Whatever it is, it (you) will keep you reactive.

To illustrate, consider what happens as you balance your budget each week. When you really take the time to examine where your money is going, you'll likely be surprised to learn how much you're doing wrong versus right. This increased awareness of another you—the one in the past that spent frivolously—will make the present you more vigilant and the future you more cautious the next time an opportunity arises to do so again.

A Beautiful View

One of the buzzwords in the corporate culture is the word *paradigm*. In simple terms, a paradigm is akin to a lens through which we "see"—and thus perceive—the world around us. Whenever the lens (paradigm) changes, so does the way we see the world. But more often, it's the world that changes first—providing new (often contradictory) information that, in turn, impacts how reliable we may consider the lens (paradigm) to be. Thus, abandoning one lens and adopting another produces a *paradigm shift*.

Tracking and evaluating goal-related data and witnessing subsequent progress will create a similar shift of understanding where you'll begin to see things with "new eyes." It's the epiphany or "a-ha" moment where things begin to click and you can see this is all working.

In fairness, it will take some time to fathom the progress and resulting meaning produced by your hard work. Paradigm shifts won't occur overnight. Because action so often exists at the margins, it's hard to see the entire forest with your nose against the bark of the trees. But the benefit of tracking and evaluating is that doing so will offer you a "satellite view"—and hence a big-picture, forest-size comprehension—of what your efforts have led to.

More than likely, the view will be beautiful.

Growth

Keep in mind that success is not only incremental; it's cumulative as well. In other words, what you achieve today will be "banked" in a way that further increases your ability to achieve tomorrow. Each "little victory," no matter how small, affirms, teaches, and instills greater confidence. Thus you boost your chances of success with each next objective as well as every future goal.

Like a boulder rolling down a hill, you'll gain more and more momentum. Success begets success.

Mapmaking

And then... you'll be done. As you manage to complete the final task of your final objective, you ought to recognize your achievement and properly celebrate the accomplishment. Congratulations—you did it!

But beyond the satisfaction of a goal achieved, the personal goal experience provides an added benefit—personal development. Life is just as much about *that* journey as the destination. If success lies on the far side of failure, perhaps it's self-development that lies on the far side of success.

Just like your physical growth, your personal development within the context of a goal will eventually come to an end. What once illuminated will soon fade, what once tasted sweet will now seem stale. But the beauty of life is that a destination is nothing more than a point on a map. As the mapmaker, you have the liberty—some might say the duty—to chart new courses and experience the inevitable growth and satisfaction they will yield. New goals, new beginnings—perhaps more ambitious in the same arena or perhaps something totally different—kindle the excitement of the inner child in each of us. Remember the tension and thrill of your first day at school and revisiting that experience as you grew older, moving each year from one classroom or school to the next? Hopefully that same feeling will resurface as you embark on each new goal's course (and if it does, you'll know your ship is sailing in the right direction).

The fact is that self-development is cyclical like every year's seasons, symbolizing a regenerative turn of the wheel of life along with wisdom and enrichment and the joy of a new challenge and unlimited possibilities, from beginning to end to beginning *ad infinitum*.

T.S. Elliot captured this spirit in his poem *Little Gidding*, where he said:

> We shall not cease from exploration
> And the end of all our exploring
> Will be to arrive where we started
> And know the place for the first time.

AFTERWORD

As you master the practices I've just described, I hope you gain new perspective and discover new meaning. Remember, you are endowed with the precious gifts of life and life's opportunities and—to paraphrase Richard Bach—your only obligation in this lifetime is to live up to your potential.

Gratitude, perhaps the most humble of qualities, sums up this perspective. Be grateful every day, show gratitude every day. Gratitude is the essence of the goaltending philosophy, which asserts that you are capable of achieving your dream as long as you're willing to accept responsibility for it; to engage in that which is meaningful; to be a dreamer but remain grounded enough to act on those dreams; and to have the maturity to collect, reflect, and correct along the way.

Achieving success with your goals may not be easy, but if you show gratitude by pursuing growth and self-development in the face of life's obstacles—whether it be growth in the arena of fitness, finance, career, or beyond—you'll have earned the satisfaction of knowing you made a difference in this world, in this lifetime.

What else could be more cause for joy?

REFERENCES AND FURTHER READING

<u>Books</u>

The 4-Hour Workweek — Timothy Ferriss
Getting Things Done — David Allen
Managing Oneself — Peter Drucker
The Now Habit — Neil Fiore
The 7 Habits of Highly Effective People — Stephen Covey
Smart Choices — John Hammond, Ralph Keeney, and Howard Raiffa
Speaking of Journalism — William Zinsser
The Success Principles — Jack Canfield
Thinking on Paper — V.A. Howard and J.H. Barton
A Touch of Wonder — Arthur Gordon
The Truth About You — Marcus Buckingham
The Ultimate Secret to Getting Absolutely Everything You Want — Mike Hernacki
The War of Art — Steven Pressfield
What Type Am I? — Renee Baron

<u>Audio</u>

How to Set and Achieve Goals — Brian Tracy
Unlimited Power — Anthony Robbins

<u>Online</u>

16 Rules for Success in Business and Life in General
(source: *http://www.bobparsons.me/bp_16_rules.php*) — Bob Parsons